Under Wraps
The Gift We Never Expected

Devotional

Under Wraps
The Gift We Never Expected

Book
978-1-4267-9373-8
978-1-6308-8296-9 (Large Print)
Also available as an eBook

Leader Guide
978-1-4267-9375-2
Also available as an eBook

DVD
978-1-4267-9378-3

Devotional
978-1-4267-9376-9
Also available as an eBook

Children's Leader Guide
978-1-4267-9381-3

Youth Study Book
978-1-4267-9379-0
Also available as an eBook

Worship Planning
978-1-4267-9382-0 (Flash Drive)
978-1-6308-8069-9 (Download)

Under Wraps

The Gift We Never Expected

Jessica LaGrone
Andy Nixon
Rob Renfroe
Ed Robb

Devotional
Jenny Youngman

Abingdon Press
Nashville

UNDER WRAPS:
THE GIFT WE NEVER EXPECTED - DEVOTIONAL

Copyright © 2014 by Abingdon Press
All rights reserved.

This book is printed on elemental chlorine-free paper.

ISBN 978-1-4267-9376-9

14 15 16 17 18 19 20 21 22 23—10 9 8 7 6 5 4 3 2 1

MANUFACTURED IN THE UNITED STATES OF AMERICA

Contents

Introduction

The four weeks of Advent are a time to slow down in a season often characterized by busyness and activity. If we're not careful, shopping sprees and parties and special events can cause us to lose sight of the real story of Christmas—God's ultimate gift to us.

That first Sunday in Advent reminds us that the story is not about our shopping stress or celebratory activities but about God's stepping down into our world to know us, to love us, and to save us. The greatest story in the history of the world is true! God is the Great Gift-giver, and his most precious gift is Jesus, the Savior of the world.

Imagine the most special gift you have ever given. What was the gift? What was the occasion? Who was the recipient? How did the recipient react to the gift? How did you feel watching this person open the gift?

Now imagine that God has prepared a gift with great joy and care for you and for me. God has made a way for us to be with him forever, and he is full of excitement to give us this gift. God has prepared us for this gift, has wrapped it up perfectly, and is waiting to give it to us.

Giving gifts is great fun. Choosing just the right gift for just the right loved one, wrapping the item beautifully, and giving the gift in hopes of blessing someone is a wonderful thing.

Surely this is how God watches as we receive the baby born in a manger in Bethlehem. God waits with eager anticipation to see our reaction and our joy.

As we prepare to receive this amazing gift, the season of Advent gives us time to reflect and pray, inviting God to work in our hearts. These devotions are meant to help you carve out that time with God and reflect on his character.

The Daily Readings

The four weeks of devotions are divided into the four themes of *Under Wraps: The Gift We Never Expected:*

- God Is Expectant
- God Is Dangerous
- God Is Jealous
- God Is Faithful

Each day of Advent, you are invited to read the printed Scripture, reflect on the devotion, and spend time in prayer asking God to do a new work in your heart this season. As we explore these four characteristics of God, we'll discover that Jesus—God "under wraps"—came to rescue and redeem us so that we could fully know God and be known by him. What a priceless gift—to be known by the God of the universe!

Expect to be changed by the Great Gift-giver this Advent. Open your heart to receive the Gift and grab hold of the hope he brings.

WEEK 1
God Is Expectant

1.

Great Expectations

For to us a child is born,
to us a son is given,
and the government will be on his shoulders.
And he will be called
Wonderful Counselor, Mighty God,
Everlasting Father, Prince of Peace.
Of the greatness of his government and peace
there will be no end.
He will reign on David's throne
and over his kingdom,
establishing and upholding it
with justice and righteousness
from that time on and forever.
The zeal of the LORD Almighty
will accomplish this.

Isaiah 9:6-7

Talk about great expectations. God's people had waited and waited and waited some more for the coming of the promised Messiah. They had believed, hoped, and looked with expectation for generations. And generation after generation, there was no sign of the awaited Savior.

The Israelites expected a king as described by Isaiah. On his shoulders would be the government—a kingdom. He would reign on a throne and uphold justice and righteousness in the land. Imagine generations of Israelites looking, expecting, and anticipating the coming of the King of kings. They had expectations of royalty riding in with horses and chariots.

Now, fast forward to Bethlehem and the birth of Jesus. The long-awaited King was coming. How does one receive a king? With grandeur, pomp, and circumstance? With feasts and parties? Shouldn't they be having planning meetings and preparing for his arrival?

No, parties and royal ceremonies would not be the way this King entered the world. Instead, this baby King came humbly and quietly in a small town without a royal parade. This King would lay low for years, waiting until the Spirit led him to proclaim his message. Not quite what God's people had expected.

Many of us have a problem with expectation adjustment. We have a hard time switching gears when what we thought was going to happen isn't what actually happens. Often we focus too much on our unmet expectations so that we miss out on the joy of many moments.

Sometimes we do this with God. We think he will show up at a certain time in a certain way in our lives, and what we think should happen doesn't. In these moments, we have to regroup and remember that God always shows up at just the right time and place. It doesn't always happen as we imagined, but the gift of God's presence in our lives has never been absent. When we look for a royal word from the sky, he often comes as a whisper in the quiet of the night.

We know from reading the Gospels that God's people had a hard time receiving Jesus as the Messiah because he was not what they thought he would be and the situation was not what they had planned or prepared for. Some regrouped and remembered that God shows up on his own time and in his own way. Others could not make the adjustment.

How will we receive the news of the awaited Prince of Peace this season? Can we allow God to enter into our lives in his own way? Can we expect to encounter him even if the situation isn't what we planned or prepared for?

In the Advent narrative God is like an expectant father ready to tell the whole world the good news of his Son's birth. This good news will change our hearts and our lives forever. With great expectation, let's invite God to show up and do a work in us this Advent.

Prayer Focus

How will you be open to encountering God, no matter how or when he shows up?

2.

Where Is Your Heart?

At that time Mary got ready and hurried to a town in the hill country of Judea, where she entered Zechariah's home and greeted Elizabeth. When Elizabeth heard Mary's greeting, the baby leaped in her womb, and Elizabeth was filled with the Holy Spirit. In a loud voice she exclaimed: "Blessed are you among women, and blessed is the child you will bear! But why am I so favored, that the mother of my Lord should come to me? As soon as the sound of your greeting reached my ears, the baby in my womb leaped for joy. Blessed is she who has believed that the Lord would fulfill his promises to her!"

Luke 1:39-45

"Let every heart prepare him room" we sing together in church or hum along with the Christmas music played in the stores for shoppers. Part of the work of waiting in Advent is to make space in your heart for the Christ child, to create margin in your life so there is space to receive and experience him as if for the first time.

Consider the expectant mother making preparations for her baby to arrive—the doctor visits, the nursery, the items in the dresser drawers, the diapers, the car seat, the stroller—all physical work to be done to welcome baby. Even still, in her heart she is pondering this life in her belly. She is wondering what he or she will be like. She is expecting to have her life radically shaken up by this little one. She expects to become a whole new version of herself. This new mom is making room in her life and in her heart for her precious child.

Advent brings us this kind of expectancy and work of preparation. We get ready for the celebration of Christ's birth with parties, concerts, baking, decorations, family traditions, and giving. All the while, in our hearts we clear away the things that have crowded out the space belonging to Jesus. We ponder what this newborn King means for our lives and our world.

Part of Mary's preparation was to visit her cousin Elizabeth. Elizabeth was also pregnant with her own version of a miracle baby. She was older than Mary and spoke into Mary's life a word of hope and confirmation that God was indeed at work in both of them. With all the preparation that needed to occur for the arrival of their babies, they took some time just to be together, to wonder at this work of God, and to soak in the miracle of it all.

We may not feel an urgent need to run to a relative, but in this season we should take a moment to think about our "Elizabeths." Who are your trusted confidants to whom you run with great news or deep sadness? Give thanks to God for these people and consider how you might play the role of mentor and encourager to others. How can you celebrate together the amazing things God is doing in your lives?

Mary and Elizabeth were about to experience extreme life changes. Their babies were going shake up everything they ever thought about who they were, what they were about, and what God was doing in them and in the world. What if we approached Advent with the same expectancy?

Just like Mary, we are shaken up when Christ comes into our lives—everything changes! The birth of the Christ-child didn't just change Mary's life, it changed our lives too. God broke into the human world in a radical way in order to make radical changes in us. And just as Elizabeth's baby leaped in her womb when Mary arrived, so our hearts leap with joy during Advent in anticipation of all that God is doing.

How is your heart preparing room for the newborn King this Advent? How can you change the rhythm of the season from busyness to expectancy, watching and waiting to see the ways that God is at work in you?

Prayer Focus
How can you prepare and create room in your heart for more of Jesus?

3.

The Image of the Invisible

The Son is the image of the invisible God, the firstborn over all creation. For in him all things were created: things in heaven and on earth, visible and invisible, whether thrones or powers or rulers or authorities; all things have been created through him and for him. He is before all things, and in him all things hold together.

Colossians 1:15-17

Often called The Christ Hymn, this passage of Scripture reveals so much about the expectant nature of God. God is not a distant, inactive being just sitting in heaven's living room and observing humans for fun. God looks with expectant eyes and a heart of love as he gives his precious Gift to the world.

The Son, the image of the invisible God, was there at the creation of the world—the world was created through him. And God waited until it was just the right time to send him into our world to be one of us. God must have been giddy with excitement knowing that, finally, we could see him with our own eyes. God would literally put on flesh to make "his dwelling among us" (John 1:14).

For so long, God's people had wanted to see God. They had asked for signs and kings and prophets. How they must have longed for Immanuel. And here he came through God's servant Mary, the sign for all the people of God's love, affection, and plan for their salvation.

Even now don't we beg God for signs and someone to say, "This is from God"? We search the Internet, ask our friends, and read endless books when all the while God says, "If you want to know where I am or what I am about, look to Jesus."

As we await the Christmas celebration this year, maybe instead of looking for joy or peace in parties and gifts, we can look more closely to Jesus. Maybe we should scour the words of Jesus, looking for the whisper of God that speaks deeply to our hearts the words we desperately need to hear.

God is giddy with excitement to bring you joy. God is over the moon to show you his plan to be with you forever. God is full of expectant joy for you to gaze on the invisible image of himself. God is thrilled to reveal himself to you.

What if we were as excited to receive Jesus as God was to send him to us? Are we receiving Jesus a little more every Christmas celebration, or have we outgrown the joy of the season? Advent brings with it the reminder that hope is alive and that love is real. No matter how much we outgrow the excitement of Christmas morning, we can't outgrow our need for more of Jesus in our lives.

As God looks on you with excitement this Advent season, may you share his excitement by receiving anew the gift of his only beloved Son.

Prayer Focus
Are you excited to receive this precious gift from God?

4.

He Has Done Great Things

And Mary said:

"My soul glorifies the Lord
    and my spirit rejoices in God my Savior,
for he has been mindful
    of the humble state of his servant.
From now on all generations will call me blessed,
    for the Mighty One has done great things for me—
    holy is his name.
His mercy extends to those who fear him,
    from generation to generation.
He has performed mighty deeds with his arm;
    he has scattered those who are proud in their
    inmost thoughts.
He has brought down rulers from their thrones
    but has lifted up the humble.
He has filled the hungry with good things
    but has sent the rich away empty.
He has helped his servant Israel,
    remembering to be merciful

> *to Abraham and his descendants forever,*
> *just as he promised our ancestors."*

Luke 1:46-55

Every mark on the timeline of our lives represents a period of life with its own special events and memories. Many of us associate songs with these periods in our lives. Maybe you remember the song that played when you first met your spouse or the song you sang as you held your newborn baby, or perhaps there are songs that take you back to high school or college.

Songs can move us, take us to a different space in our minds, and express thoughts for which we cannot find words. Sometimes the only appropriate action in a situation is to sing a song—either a song of joy and celebration or a song of grief, lament, and hope.

Throughout the Bible, we see God's people singing songs of praise for the great things God has done for them. The psalms are full of songs of praise as well as songs of lament. Songs help us share the thoughts of our hearts with God when words are hard to find.

The Gospel of Luke gives us songs from Zechariah, Simeon, the angels, and Mary. Mary's song not only marks a major event in her life—carrying and giving birth to the Son of God—it also declares a new reality for her and for generations to come. God's promise no longer is something that is coming; it's here and now!

The song of Mary is praise for what God has done in her, but it's also a declaration of what God will do generation after generation. The song names the activity of God and assumes a current reality of God's action. Every promise God has made is coming true. God is doing what he promised to do. The Messiah is coming to change everything, and we are the recipients of that good news. Mary invites us into her song as recipients of God's mercy.

As we spend this week considering that God is expectant, Mary's song reveals for us that God is actively involved in the lives of his beloved children. He expects to act. He is ready with mercy and his perfect provision. He loves to bless the humble and lift up the lowly. He honors his covenant and fulfills his promises.

What is happening in your life this Advent? What causes you to sing a song of praise for God's work in your life? Maybe you are among the lowly this season and need God to lift you up. Maybe you are among the hungry and need physical or spiritual food to sustain you. Maybe you have seen the promises of God fulfilled and are quick to praise God. Wherever you are and whatever your path this Advent, hear this promise from sweet Mary: "[God's] mercy extends to those who fear him, / from generation to generation" (Luke 1:50). This promise is for you and for me. We can sing in the midst of great trial or great joy because God will always lift up the lowly. He will always be in the business of doing great things in and through and for us.

Sing with Mary, Zechariah, and the heavenly hosts, praising God for all he has done. Ours is a song of hope, expectation, and promise. Ours is a song of great things and of a great God. Will you join in the song?

Prayer Focus

Write a psalm of praise for all that God has done in your life.

5.
God's Party

On this mountain the LORD Almighty will prepare
a feast of rich food for all peoples,
a banquet of aged wine—
the best of meats and the finest of wines.
On this mountain he will destroy
the shroud that enfolds all peoples,
the sheet that covers all nations;
he will swallow up death forever.
The Sovereign LORD will wipe away the tears
from all faces;
he will remove his people's disgrace
from all the earth,
The LORD has spoken.
In that day they will say,

"Surely this is our God;
we trusted in him, and he saved us.
This is the LORD, we trusted in him;
let us rejoice and be glad in his salvation."

Isaiah 25:6-9

Don't you just love a good party? There is nothing like warm hospitality, a buffet of wonderful food and drinks, and a gathering of people who are enjoying their time together. When all the arrangements are taken care of and the feast is provided, the guests are free to enjoy, celebrate, and relax.

This passage from Isaiah describes the feast that God expectantly and excitedly sets for all peoples. This feast represents the kind of party God loves to throw in which the oppressed and torn down feel like royalty—and even become royalty! Yesterday we praised with Mary that God lifts up the lowly and gives food to the hungry. Today we see that God doesn't just give the lowly a pat on the back and send the hungry away with the standard-issue PB&J. No, God sets a feast, hosting an elaborate party for the lowly and the hungry and the oppressed. Those who have been on the outside of society, the least among people, the downtrodden and brokenhearted—these are the ones God invites to this party. The Lord loves to bless his beloved with a feast.

It is right to throw parties at Christmas to celebrate the great work of God. We plan for, shop, and cook an extravagant meal; bring out the good dishes and set a lovely table; gather with loved ones; and exchange gifts not because Santa Claus is coming to town but because Love came down at Christmas. Love came down to swallow up death and to wipe away every tear. Love came down to remove our disgrace and to remove the veil that separated God from his people. We party because Love has come. Often in the busyness we can forget the reason for it all. Love has come, friends. Have a party and celebrate!

Sometimes during the holiday season our festivities expand to donating food and clothing, sponsoring families who can't afford their own celebrations, and sending boxes of gifts to children around the world who may not otherwise receive a gift. We extend our feasts to poor and needy persons we may never meet and help others experience the season. We are noble in our human efforts to bless others. But what would it look like for our holiday festivities to include the poor, the needy, the distressed, and the brokenhearted in ways that reflect God's feast—with all peoples gathered around the same table together? While we donate worn-out or out-of-style clothing and buy cheap food items to donate, could we also prepare a rich feast and sit at the table together with those we mean to serve? Instead of passing on our unwanted goods, could we lavish someone with just what he or she has wanted? How might God's feast image in Isaiah help you plan your giving and celebrating this year?

We party not only because Love has come but also because, though there are troubles in this world, God has defeated death. Death is swallowed up in Jesus. This newborn King we await will be our peace in the midst of whatever worldly storm comes our way. He is the One we've waited for. Isaiah's words point us to the hope in Jesus' coming and dying and rising again. Love has come; hope is here. Let's have a feast!

Prayer Focus

Memorize this verse and let your celebrations reflect your joy:

> "This is the LORD, we trusted in him;
>   let us rejoice and be glad in his salvation."
>
> Isaiah 25:9b

6.

The Lord Is Near

The Lord is near. Do not be anxious about anything, but in every situation, by prayer and petition, with thanksgiving, present your requests to God. And the peace of God, which transcends all understanding, will guard your hearts and your minds in Christ Jesus.

Philippians 4:5b-7

If any time of year can be considered anxiety producing, it surely could be the compressed seasons of Thanksgiving and Christmas. Somehow the break between the two holidays has evaporated into twenty-four-hour sales and a sad display of consumerism. Now we have one big, long holiday that starts sometime after Halloween and doesn't end until New Year's Day. We're encouraged to buy, buy, buy for the sake of the economy. There's always new technology to acquire, some new style of clothing that is a must-have, and the annual "in" gift we must have this season. Then there are the family dynamics and unmet expectations, not to mention the desire for magical moments and perfect photo opportunities. The quest for the perfect Christmas can be quite anxiety inducing!

If the cultural pressures to buy stuff and to celebrate aren't enough, a real and deeper anxiety defines the season for many people. How sad that a season meant to induce hope and joy is often reduced to anxious thoughts related to shopping lists and Christmas dinner seating charts. Oftentimes what gets lost among the frenetic nature of November and December is our attention to the real hurts and sadness we carry inside, masking them with a smile as we tackle our to-do lists. Yet often underneath our outward stress lies a real struggle with loneliness, depression, loss, grief, or a broken heart. Sadly, some among us suffer silently either because we are too busy to notice or we fear breaking an unspoken "holiday happiness" code.

Between our outward anxiety and the inner sadness that often accompanies the holidays, these words from Philippians are like a salve: "The Lord is near" (4:5b). He is with us. We are not alone. We can bring him our cares, our fears, our worries, and our requests. He invites us to hand them over.

What a gift to claim the season of Advent and protest the frantic pace of the culture. Advent calls us out of anxiousness and into excited anticipation. We know that the King is coming and that he has overcome the world. Why would we be anxious about anything when the Overcomer holds our cares in his hands?

And what do we make of this peace that surpasses understanding and that will guard our hearts? Can it really be that if we rejoice in the Lord and bring to him everything that causes anxiety in us, he will give us a peace we can't understand? A peace that will guard our hearts from despair? That is exactly what these words from Philippians teach us.

God waits expectantly to hear our prayers and to respond in love.

The anxiety of our culture is a facade. We can push against this anxiety by laying it before the Lord and inviting his peace to guard our hearts from the frenzy of the season. We can slow down, give our worries to Jesus, and rejoice that God is at the ready with a perfect peace.

Prayer Focus

What anxieties are you dealing with? Give them to Jesus.

7.

We Wait for You

But the eyes of the LORD are on those who fear him,
on those whose hope is in his unfailing love.
to deliver them from death
and keep them alive in famine.

We wait in hope for the LORD;
he is our help and our shield.
In him our hearts rejoice,
for we trust in his holy name.
May your unfailing love be with us, LORD,
even as we put our hope in you.

Psalm 33:18-22

Are you feeling far removed from abundant life? Rejoice in this truth: the Lord can be trusted with all your circumstances. If you are hungry, remember that Jesus is the Bread of Life. If you are thirsty, remember that Jesus is the Living Water. If you are broken, remember that Jesus is the Great Healer. If you are scared or scarred, remember that Jesus is the Great Defender and Restorer. In this season of expectation and anticipation of all that God has done and is doing, remember that God watches over us through eyes of love.

After many years of celebrating Christmas, we can become numb to the joy of the season. Sometimes we find ourselves just going through the motions. But God watches full of expectation to meet us with his faithful love. His eyes are always on us, and his heart is always full of love toward us. What a gift to know and serve a God who is so good!

So what are you expecting this season? What are you waiting for God to do in your life? What changes are you inviting God to make? Can you wait actively, fully expecting God to complete a good work in you? God has planned from the beginning of time to save you, redeem you, and make you his own. God is for you and working for your good.

Much like a young child who wakes with excitement several times during the night before Christmas, hoping that it's finally time to open the presents and enjoy all of the activities of the day, God longs for us to wake up our hearts toward him— confident that he will meet us with faithful love, provision, and blessings. Children hope with full expectation that their hopes will be realized. How much more, when we put our hope in the Lord, can we expect to see our hopes met in the coming of the Christ child? As the carol says, "The hopes and fears of all the years are met in Thee tonight."[1] May we wait with joy-filled expectation as our hopes and fears are met in Jesus.

Prayer Focus
Lord, let your faithful love surround us, because we wait for you.

Week 2
God Is Dangerous

1.

The Danger of Light

"For God so loved the world that he gave his one and only Son, that whoever believes in him shall not perish but have eternal life. For God did not send his Son into the world to condemn the world, but to save the world through him. Whoever believes in him is not condemned, but whoever does not believe stands condemned already because they have not believed in the name of God's one and only Son. This is the verdict: Light has come into the world, but people loved darkness instead of light because their deeds were evil. Everyone who does evil hates the light, and will not come into the light for fear that their deeds will be exposed. But whoever lives by the truth comes into the light, so that it may be seen plainly that what they have done has been done in the sight of God."

John 3:16-21

Many times when we think of dangerous places, we associate darkness with them—dark alleys, shadow lands, nighttime on the city streets. When the morning light comes, the evils of the night hide from the brightness of the sun. It makes sense that crime would favor the darkness where it is easier to hide or make a getaway.

But the light described in the Gospel of John is not one that can be escaped. Hiding from the Light is impossible because the Light not only exposes evil but also overcomes it completely. The Light came to pierce through the darkness so that people would experience the freedom of living in the Light.

However, the Scripture says that "people loved darkness instead of light because their deeds were evil" (v. 19). It's easy to point the finger at "those people" and wonder what is wrong with them. Why don't they accept the light and love of Jesus? Why don't they get that God sent his only Son into the world to save us? What could possibly be better about darkness as opposed to light?

Before we get too comfortable with our condemnation of "those people," think about how difficult it is sometimes to let go of bitterness that you rehash just for the sake of being mad. Or what about the gossip that all your friends are talking about, the little white lie, the apathetic prayer life, or the hoarding of gifts or resources or money? Don't we all have a difficult time letting the Light blot out those places of darkness we sneak off to when we think no one is watching?

The danger of following God isn't just about giving sacrificially or saying yes to that far-off missionary adventure. Sometimes the dangerous part of a life with God is the fact that "in him there is no darkness at all" (1 John 1:5). It feels dangerous or unsafe to let the God of the universe see into our broken human souls. What will he do when he sees how we really are? Could he still love us when he knows the real us? With God, there is nowhere to hide our true colors, nowhere to hold on to our beloved resentments, nowhere to shove our baggage. God sees it all, and that can feel a little scary.

But there is good news—no, great news! We do not have to scurry around, looking for a place to hide. God doesn't send the light of the world to condemn us. He doesn't turn on the light to catch us in the act. Instead, God sends the light of the world to overcome the darkness. He comes to free us from its hold on us. He comes to expose us to the light. For those who long for the truth and the light, what a difference a sunrise makes! Instead of darkness, we can live in light because of the amazing gift God gave us in his only Son: "God so loved the world that he gave his only Son, so that everyone who believes in him won't perish but will have eternal life" (John 3:16 CEB).

Prayer Focus
What parts of yourself do you try to hide from God? Invite him to shine a light into your heart and free you from any sin you can't let go of.

2.

Dangerous but Good

The L*ORD* *had said to Abram, "Go from your country, your people and your father's household to the land I will show you.*

> *"I will make you into a great nation,*
> *and I will bless you;*
> *I will make your name great,*
> *and you will be a blessing.*
> *I will bless those who bless you,*
> *and whoever curses you I will curse;*
> *and all peoples on earth*
> *will be blessed through you."*

So Abram went as the L*ORD* *had told him; and Lot went with him. Abram was seventy-five years old when he set out from Harran.*

Genesis 12:1-4

In case there was ever an assumption that a life with God would be perfect, safe, or predictable, early in the Bible we find the story of Abraham and Sarah. Abraham had made a pretty good life for himself and his family. He owned property and had acquired a bit of wealth. Sure, he had wanted a child with his beloved Sarah, but at his age he had given up on the idea. He was probably content to enjoy the rest of his years in full view of all that he had accomplished—that is, until God called to him and asked him to go to a yet undetermined land. His instructions were simply to leave his homeland and go. The promise was that God would bless him and make him a blessing for generations to come.

Abraham and Sarah started their journey into the danger of the unknown with faith in God's promise, though along the way they would try to expedite God's plan out of fear or impatience. When their caravan spent some time in Egypt, Abraham lied to the Egyptians about who Sarah was. He told them she was his sister instead of admitting that she was his wife. In Abraham's opinion, Sarah was much too beautiful for him to risk the truth. Abraham sensed a danger that the Egyptians might kill him to get to Sarah. In telling them that she was his sister, he thought he was protecting himself and gaining access to provision in a time of famine.

Later on in their story, we find Abraham and Sarah growing too impatient with God's timing and deciding to take the matter into their own hands. God had promised them a baby, and since Sarah had not yet conceived, she devised a plan for Abraham to have a child with her servant Hagar. Of course, things didn't go too smoothly!

Feeling out of control of a situation can feel dangerous, can't it? We like to be in control. We like to plan. We like to make arrangements. We like to know what to expect. But God had told Abraham and Sarah to wait for his timing.

Because they couldn't wait, they experienced an unnecessary amount of grief and turmoil.

Through it all, though, God was with Abraham and Sarah. He had a plan and a call for them. It would not be a safe journey, but it would be a good one. It would not be free from danger, but they would see God's protection and provision. It would not include an exact itinerary of where to go, what to do, and what to say; but God promised to be ever present.

The same is true for us. A life with God is not free from danger, but a life with God is always good. Our journey will not always be safe, but God promises to go with us. God will not hand us a dossier of travel plans; but he will guide us, one step at a time, into his will for us.

This Advent, consider how you have known God's presence or protection when you faced danger. Like Abraham, we are blessed to be a blessing. Blessing others sometimes can be a rocky and unsure path, but we have the promise of God's presence and protection. When God calls and we say yes, we walk into his good will for our lives.

Jesus came into this world amid danger. It was dangerous for Mary to carry a child as an unwed mother. It was dangerous for Joseph to stay with Mary. It was dangerous to give birth in a barn. It was dangerous to hide the baby from Herod. But God was up to something and would see it through.

When God is up to something, it may not be safe; but we can know with confidence that God will always see us through.

Prayer Focus

How has God been faithful to you as you have said yes to his call?

3.

God Cares for You

Now Moses was tending the flock of Jethro his father-in-law, the priest of Midian, and he led the flock to the far side of the wilderness and came to Horeb, the mountain of God. There the angel of the LORD appeared to him in flames of fire from within a bush. Moses saw that though the bush was on fire it did not burn up. So Moses thought, "I will go over and see this strange sight—why the bush does not burn up."

When the LORD saw that he had gone over to look, God called to him from within the bush, "Moses! Moses!"

And Moses said, "Here I am."

"Do not come any closer," God said. "Take off your sandals, for the place where you are standing is holy ground." Then he said, "I am the God of your father, the God of Abraham, the God of Isaac and the God of Jacob." At this, Moses hid his face, because he was afraid to look at God.

Exodus 3:1-6

It's no wonder that Moses was afraid. He was minding his own business, caring for his father's flock, when he noticed a fire. As if a bush on fire wasn't enough cause for alarm, a voice called from the bush to Moses and said his name. A talking, burning bush! Imagine what Moses must have thought—he must have assumed he had lost his mind. But he approached the flame until God called out, "Don't come any closer!" If we wonder if God's presence can be dangerous, here is our answer.

But even in the danger, don't miss the care that God took with Moses. God told Moses to take off his shoes, stand back, and recognize the holiness of the encounter. Even the ground around the bush had become holy in the presence of God, and God invited Moses to take it all in.

Most cinematic displays of this scene portray the voice of God in a deep, authoritative voice, almost yelling at Moses. But I wonder if the voice was more caring than stern. God was saying, "Moses, I'm God. I'm dangerous. Let me teach you how you can come close."

Moses was familiar with danger. His life began in danger and was framed by danger until the end. God called him to do things that were beyond his ability, but God provided what he lacked. God gave him strength to endure what would come.

Let's walk through the highlights of Moses' journey to discover the way God provided even in the midst of danger.

Moses was born at a time when the Pharaoh had ordered the death of newborn Hebrew boys. In complete desperation, his mother placed him in a basket in the river in hopes that he would drift to safety. He ended up being rescued by the Pharaoh's daughter and cared for in the Pharaoh's home by their maidservant—who just happened to be Moses' mother. I can imagine Moses' mother partly feeling relief from the panic of what to do and partly waiting for the other shoe to drop.

Moses grew up in the palace and found some favor there. But it wouldn't last. In a rage of anger, Moses killed an Egyptian man who was abusing a Hebrew. Pharaoh found out about it and wanted to kill Moses, so Moses became a man on the run. At this point, God provided a refuge in the home of some women Moses had rescued, and there he also found his wife.

When God found Moses tending his father-in-law's flock, God called him to what appeared to be still more danger. It was not safe to walk up to the Egyptian king and demand for the slaves to be set free. Basically Moses was threatening him, telling him to either let the Hebrews go or to see the power of their God unleashed.

Moses wanted to trust God but still had some anxiety. He was worried about being taken seriously and about whether or not he would be believed. So God provided care in the form of a sign and a partner. God would turn Moses' staff into a snake if he needed a sign. And God would let Moses' brother Aaron go with him to speak for him. It was a dangerous journey, but God cared for him every step of the way.

Moses' story affirms that a life with God does not equal safety. Instead, a life with God is an invitation to bravery. God calls us to things that seem beyond our capacity. He invites us to come close to him, to feel the holy ground under our feet, to hear his word, and to receive his call. There is not a promise of safety, but there is, most definitely, a promise of care.

Wherever God leads, he will care for you every step of the way.

Prayer Focus
When have you sensed God's care in the midst of danger?

4.

Run to God

The word of the LORD came to Jonah son of Amittai: "Go to the great city of Nineveh and preach against it, because its wickedness has come up before me."

But Jonah ran away from the LORD and headed for Tarshish.

Jonah 1:1-3a

Remember when you were young and your parents would ask you to do something you didn't want to do, and you would do the exact opposite, partly out of spite and partly out of arrogance? Or maybe you're a parent now and have been on the other side of this, watching your children do the exact opposite of your instruction. We can all relate to the "I'm-going-to-do-the-opposite-of-what-you're asking" urge that swells within us when we're feeling challenged or a little full of ourselves. Maybe that's why Jonah's story is so easy to relate to.

Jonah received a word from the Lord to go to Ninevah. So what did he do? He hopped a ship in the opposite direction. He ran as fast as he could the other way. As we know on this side of Jonah's story, this did not serve him well. His choice meant that he wound up on a sinking ship in the middle of a stormy sea. Then, when the crew threw him overboard in hope that God would calm the storm, he found himself in the belly of a big fish. There he was fully alive, seaweed wrapped around his head, experiencing the inner-workings of a fish's belly, and wondering if perhaps he maybe should have listened to God's instructions instead of trying to escape.

In Jonah's defense, Ninevah was a dangerous, God-hating place. They had lost all sense of right and wrong and were hostile to the idea of godliness. God had asked Jonah to walk into a city known for evil and to tell them to change their ways. He was to walk the streets declaring that God was about to show them how he felt about their actions. It's not hard to relate to Jonah's fear about this instruction from God.

Eventually Jonah went to Ninevah and did as God had asked. You might not think that the Ninevites would listen to Jonah, but they did. They fasted and prayed and changed their ways in hopes that God would change his mind. And he did!

Jonah was enraged at God for changing his mind. He expected to go to Ninevah, give them the what-for, and watch as God brought his wrath. He did not think it was fair for God to change plans after he had promised the destruction of the city because of their evil acts. He didn't want them to receive any of God's goodness after so many years of wickedness.

Jonah experienced firsthand the dangerous road of following God. He knew there was danger in saying yes to God's call, and he experienced the danger of saying no as well. And when, in his melodramatic fashion, he declared that he would rather die than see God show mercy to Ninevah, Jonah learned that there was also the danger of not getting the outcome he expected, even after saying yes to God.

As we follow God more closely and listen for his call, we have to surrender the outcome. We have to trust that his ways are good—even when we get a different ending from what we want.

Mary said yes not knowing fully what the outcome would be. Joseph didn't know what the end result of his would be. They could have run in the opposite direction, but they faithfully said yes, not fully knowing the outcome but knowing that it would be a dangerous road.

This Advent, may we say yes in full obedience to God's word to us, trusting him with the outcome.

Prayer Focus
When have you tried to run from God? When have you wished for a different outcome?

5.

The Kingdom of Heaven Has Come Near

These twelve Jesus sent out with the following instructions: "Do not go among the Gentiles or enter any town of the Samaritans. Go rather to the lost sheep of Israel. As you go, proclaim this message: 'The kingdom of heaven has come near.' . . .

"I am sending you out like sheep among wolves. . . .

"Do not suppose that I have come to bring peace to the earth. I did not come to bring peace, but a sword."

Matthew 10: 5-7, 16a, 34

In the middle of Matthew 10, Jesus tells his disciples to not be afraid (see verses 26-31). He has said that he is sending them as sheep among wolves; he has said that there will be snakes disguised as doves; he has said that he came to bring a sword against evil in this world; he has said that they will have to give up their lives to find them. But he tells them not to be afraid!

Don't be afraid. This sentiment appears numerous times throughout the Bible, often when God is giving an instruction to someone. Don't be afraid? You might then wonder, "What is there to fear?" In Matthew 10, Jesus tells his disciples that real discipleship is a dangerous road. He knows why they would be afraid and even spells it out for them. They will be asked to go where it feels unsafe. They will be tempted and tricked by the enemy. They will be run out of town. They will have to give up everything they know and love and that brings them security. But here is the promise: they will gain abundant, eternal life.

Don't we sometimes allow fear to rob ourselves of experiencing abundant life? We are afraid of what might happen. We are afraid of the unknown. We are afraid of new experiences. We are afraid of potential crime. We are afraid of what people will think. We are afraid of not knowing what to say. We are afraid of not having a friend. We are afraid of getting hurt.

Jesus calls to us—don't be afraid! A life with Jesus won't necessarily be safe, but true discipleship and abundant life require letting go of the fear that keeps us from following Jesus. There is trouble in this world. The enemy stands ready to trip us and cause us to ignore Jesus. There is evil and injustice and oppression. Jesus is calling his followers to bravery and to action, not to hiding out in safety.

Some would have you believe that following Jesus means health, wealth, and a long, safe life. But that misses the promise entirely. God is not safe, but God is so good. A life with God means laying down your life. A life with God means giving up your desires and surrendering to God's desires. What God does promise is his presence with you, his power at work in you, and his provision for your needs.

The kingdom of heaven has come near in the Christ child. This is the announcement we are called to shout from the rooftops and take to the world. How does your life announce the kingdom of heaven come near this Advent?

Prayer Focus

Invite God to show you how to proclaim his kingdom as you observe Advent and celebrate Christmas this year.

6.
Troubled

After Jesus was born in Bethlehem in Judea, during the time of King Herod, Magi from the east came to Jerusalem and asked, "Where is the one who has been born king of the Jews? We saw his star when it rose and have come to worship him."

When King Herod heard this, he was disturbed.

Matthew 2:1-3a

Herod was troubled because he sensed a threat to his leadership, but isn't it odd that a king would be afraid of an infant? Even if the baby grew to be an earthly king, surely Herod's reign would be over by then. Herod was known for being harsh and cruel, even killing his own wife and sons. Why would he be afraid of a baby?

Well, this baby had been prophesied about for generations. Some of Herod's constituents had been looking for this king to come for years and years. The prophecies announced that earthly kingdoms would crumble and current cultures would be turned upside down. The birth of Jesus was an announcement from heaven that change was in the air, and Herod did not like that sinking feeling in his stomach—so much so that he ordered the death of infant boys in Bethlehem.

He was right to be afraid of Jesus. It is true that Jesus would come to challenge the government, speak out on behalf of the poor and the outcasts in society, and make claims that the kingdom of heaven had come to earth. Herod may not have known what to expect with this baby Jesus, but Jesus would be more than "troubling" to the government and religious leaders of his day.

Jesus came to set things right, to flip society on its head. The people looked for a mighty Messiah born to fanfare, but they got a humble newborn king born in a stable. They thought he would march into the government offices and take over, but instead he gathered a small group, shared his vision, and let his revolution happen a little bit at a time.

Herod was right to be afraid of what Jesus could do and what he meant for Herod's leadership. Anticipating what Jesus can do to our lives can cause us some fear too. When we say yes to Jesus, we will have to lay down our right to rule our lives. We will have to give up final authority over our futures. We will have to let Jesus turn everything upside down. We will have to care about the things he cares about—poverty, oppression, injustice, freedom, pure love for God. These changes can be troubling for a moment, but not when we consider what they mean.

Because of Jesus we are promised eternal life. In Christ, we are no longer condemned for our sin in this world. Because Jesus has come, we have hope and joy in the midst of the troubles of this world. Because of Jesus we have a future full of promise.

When Jesus comes into our lives, we are not free from troubles. At first, it can be troubling to let Jesus bring changes in us—to give up control of our time and gifts. It can be troubling to release our limited power in exchange for God's power at work in us. But the changes are so worth the blessings!

What a blessing it is to put others ahead of ourselves. What a blessing it is to prioritize our lives around the things that God cares about and to see the hand of God at work. What a blessing it is to know God's presence when we are afraid. What a blessing it is to receive Jesus as King of our lives.

Have you felt troubled about giving up your power and letting God's power work in you? Have you felt troubled with the decision to let Jesus be the Lord of your life? Could you take off your crown and lay it at the feet of Jesus, inviting him to be the Lord of your life and the King of your days? Advent is the perfect time for this invitation. Invite the Prince of Peace to turn your life upside down.

Prayer Focus
How does your life reflect that Jesus is your King?

7.
Sent

"My prayer is not that you take them out of the world but that you protect them from the evil one. They are not of the world, even as I am not of it. Sanctify them by the truth; your word is truth. As you sent me into the world, I have sent them into the world."

John 17:15-18

In this chapter from the Gospel of John, we see Jesus praying for his disciples. He knows that the evil one is prowling around looking for Jesus-followers to devour. He knows they will feel pressed on every side, persecuted, put down, and abused. He knows that they have a task that is too big for them and that requires the power of God to be released in them. This is what it means to be a disciple.

But hear Jesus' affection for his followers in his prayer: "protect them" (v. 15). Life with God is dangerous and even Jesus pleads with the Father to protect his followers. Jesus shows us that his followers are sent into the world as he was—into turmoil and hostility. Jesus was God's Son, and even he was not safe from earthly death; yet he walked his road obediently, trusting God. Our road may not lead to death because of our faith, but we are called to walk a road of discipleship. Do we have a faith that stands strong in the face of danger? Do we have a dangerous faith that laughs in the face of evil and plants its feet on the power of God?

We often sanitize the Christmas story into a sweet, peaceful scene. But it wasn't free from danger, and neither is a life following after that newborn King. A life of following Jesus may require us to give sacrificially. A life of following Jesus may require us to go somewhere out of our comfort zone. A life of following Jesus may lead us to speak up on behalf of the voiceless and marginalized. A life of following Jesus may mean standing out in a culture of look-a-likes.

What is dangerous about your faith right now? If you don't sense anything big or dangerous about following Jesus, you may need to ask him if you're following closely enough. He walked into certain death on our behalf, and he invites us into a life of that kind of bravery—the kind that lays down its life for another. His light exposes the darkness in the world and within each of us. Everywhere his light shines, he overcomes darkness. Jesus sends his followers with such a power. Christ in us gives us the power to take that light and overcome the darkness in the world. Though the darkness may be dangerous, we need not fear because the Light has already overcome it.

Could you be so bold as to invite Jesus to do a dangerous work in you this season? Could you invite Jesus to send you into the world by whatever path he calls you? Can you bravely stare down the enemy with all the power of heaven on your side?

As the sun rises each day in this Advent season, may you experience an onslaught of bravery and extraordinary love to follow Jesus wherever he leads.

Prayer Focus
Invite God to send you to places where you must rely on his strength and power.

WEEK 3
God Is Jealous

1.

All We Are

"Love the Lord your God with all your heart and with all your soul and with all your strength and with all your mind'; and, 'Love your neighbor as yourself."

Luke 10:27

Part of the work of preparation in Advent is to search our hearts and look for idols that steal a part of us away from God. This week we are going to peel back the layers of the world that creep in and keep us from all-out loyalty to our God.

The best place to start the work of removing idols is with the commandment on which everything in Scripture rests. Passing the test from the legal expert, Jesus answers the question "What must I do to gain eternal life?" with a teaching upon which would rest all other mandates in the Scripture. His instruction would be called the Great Commandment. We are commanded to love God with everything we are—heart, soul, strength, and mind—and to love our neighbors as we love ourselves. With this verse Jesus reminds us what we know about God: that he is, indeed, a jealous God, that he wants all of us.

Love God with all your heart. What kinds of things do you give your heart to? Maybe you have given God everything but that one thing you just can't surrender. Maybe you reserved one little corner of your heart to bury some secret, sin, or struggle that you feel safer holding onto than letting go so that you can find out who you are without it. Whatever the thing is for each of us—be it our time, our talents, our money, our control, our pride, our families—God wants us to gather up all we have and are and lay ourselves at his feet. He wants all of us. If our hearts are devoted to anything apart from God, then we are not loving God with all our hearts.

Take a minute now to consider what might be keeping you from loving God with all your heart. Invite God to give you a clean and pure heart that is all his.

Love God with all your soul. You may have never considered what it means to love God with your soul. Often in the English language heart and soul are used to mean the same thing, so why would Jesus make a point to use both words? Consider that the soul is used to describe a person's very essence and identity. The soul is the central core within us from which we act, make decisions, and live. It is our identity, our starting point. Are our very lives wrapped up in and defined by our love for God? Is our love for God our starting point for every single act we take?

Take a minute now to reflect on this: Do you love God with all your soul—is it who you are? Tell God in this moment how much you love him. Invite him to show you how to love him more.

Love God with all your strength. To love God with all your strength is to give it all you've got. Marathoners know about using every bit of strength they can muster. They train and prepare and eat so that they may store up strength for the race. They build their muscles and endurance so that they have strength at the end of the journey. They commit to a schedule and a level of effort that will prepare them for whatever comes their way. In the same way, we love God with all our strength when we give him everything we've got—when we change our patterns, habits, schedules, and priorities because of our love for him.

Now, take a minute to reflect on loving God with your strength. Are your habits, patterns, and choices reflective of your love for God? Ask God for strength to be all out in your love for him.

Love God with all your mind. Our minds hold so much of who we are—our thoughts, our ability to reason, our imagination, our knowledge, our lessons from life experiences, our ability to process events. If our minds are not focused on God, they are quick to spiral off into ungodly places. It's no wonder that the writer of Philippians would instruct us to think about noble things, good things, true things, excellent things (Philippians 4:8). It's also no wonder that the apostle Paul would teach us that we are transformed by the renewing of our minds (Romans 12:2).

Our minds take in so many images and so much information that we are easily distracted from our love for God. In order to love God with all our minds, we have to train them, focusing and directing our thoughts through the lens of our love for God.

Think about it: how often does your mind wander off into thoughts of anger, bitterness, resentment, gossip, and even sinful desires? These thoughts are not the excellent thoughts the writer of Philippians encourages us to think about. So we have to do the work of training our minds to love God fully by studying and memorizing Scriptures, remembering and reflecting on all that God has done, meditating on God's goodness, and imagining and dreaming God-sized dreams. Finally, invite God to renew your mind, to reset your thoughts and expand your thinking. Focus your mind to make every thought filter through your love for God and God's great love for you.

Spend the rest of today reflecting on how you can live out this commandment from Jesus to love God with all your heart, soul, strength, and mind. Do the work of creating room for more of Christ in your heart and giving all of yourself to God.

Prayer Focus
What keeps me from loving God with everything I am?

2.

Good Jealousy

Do not worship any other god, for the LORD, whose name is Jealous, is a jealous God.

Exodus 34:14

In our culture's language, jealousy is the stuff of soap operas, immaturity, and worldliness. The word as we use it denotes pettiness, envy, and greed. Our culture wants us to be jealous of what others have so that we'll rush out to get whatever we need to keep up with our neighbors. And from what we see on TV and in the movies, jealousy can keep a story going!

As we know it, jealousy infers a general distrust and unhappiness. But jealousy alone is not evil, otherwise God would not have called himself Jealous. God's jealousy must be pure and holy, so what does it mean to say that God is jealous for us when our understanding of jealousy seems so petty?

First, we have to remember that not all jealousy is bad. In a marriage relationship, two people commit to faithfulness of body and mind. When one of the two has directed his or her affections away from the marriage covenant, the other is right to be jealous for his or her affection. Jealousy is the right response to the breach of faithfulness; it's a demonstration of passion, love, and commitment to the marriage.

God is jealous in the best way possible. He loves his people so much that he cannot share them with false gods. In this scene from Exodus 34, God is not expressing an angry surge of a jealous feeling. Instead, he is communicating that his name, his essence, his nature is Jealous. God tells us that *Jealous* is his name. God is high above all other gods of the world and anything that would try to compete with him for supremacy in our lives.

The crux of God's jealousy is love for us. God so loves us that he cannot allow anything else in all the world to share our hearts with him. Allowing us to give a little of our hearts to him and a little to lesser things demeans his very nature. He is jealous for us because he loves us and has our best interests in mind.

The translation of jealous in this passage is sometimes noted as zealous or having zeal. God loves us with great zeal and wants us to love him back with that same zeal. Even more than that, God wants us to love others with that same zeal—to be jealous for others to know God's love as well.

Do you love God with zeal, or do your heart and attention wander to the many lesser gods of the world? As you prepare for the Christmas celebration, have you made the focus on welcoming Jesus or on acquiring more stuff and stress? This work of preparation in Advent cuts deep to examine the state of our hearts, of our love for our God. It is not a good feeling to discover that we have taken our eyes off of God and let them gaze upon lesser things.

Ask God to give you single-mindedness in your love for him. Ask him for help to shatter the idols competing for your loyalty. God is jealous for you. God loves you with a fierce, passionate, jealous love; and this is a good, good thing.

Prayer Focus

What idols in your life try to gain your loyalty?

3.
God So Loved...

But Moses sought the favor of the Lord his God. "Lord," he said, "why should your anger burn against your people, whom you brought out of Egypt with great power and a mighty hand? Why should the Egyptians say, 'It was with evil intent that he brought them out, to kill them in the mountains and to wipe them off the face of the earth'? Turn from your fierce anger; relent and do not bring disaster on your people. Remember your servants Abraham, Isaac and Israel, to whom you swore by your own self: 'I will make your descendants as numerous as the stars in the sky and I will give your descendants all this land I promised them, and it will be their inheritance forever.'" Then the Lord relented and did not bring on his people the disaster he had threatened.

Exodus 32: 11-14

How many times God's people got it wrong! They got it wrong throughout the Scriptures, and we are still getting it wrong today. God had led his people from slavery, and they were on their way to the Promised Land. They had seen the amazing work of God; they knew that God was on their side. Yet they doubted and took matters into their own hands.

When Moses went to up the mountain to receive instructions from the Lord, he took longer than the Israelites thought he should take. They started to get nervous and to make arrangements to get some control over their situation. They began to doubt that God was really for them and decided to make some idols with their own hands. They needed to direct their loyalty somewhere, and since Moses was gone and couldn't tell them what to do, they made their own gods to worship.

You can imagine that this did not make God happy. In his righteous anger, he wanted to just start over with the human race. He was exasperated at their lack of obedience and trust. At first glance it might seem like God was vengeful and in an angry rage, but notice how Moses pleaded and God relented. Ultimately, God loved his people so much that he gave them chance after chance until, finally, he sent a Rescuer who would save us from our idolatrous inclinations once and for all.

God loves us so much. He knows that giving our affections to anything less than him will only lead to disappointment and regret. He knows that the only way to full, abundant life is in him. He knows that idol worship distracts us from his will for our lives and takes us off course. He is jealous for us—he wants the best for us. We are at our best when we put God first in our lives and make him our top priority.

To show us just how much God loves us, he sent Jesus to us. John 3:16 reminds us that God sent his only Son to the world. Jesus wasn't another messenger or prophet but God incarnate. He would be our Rescuer and Savior. Jesus would reveal to us the heart of God and ask for our hearts in return. God's jealousy for us led him to come down to live among us, to know us, and to be known by us. God has gone to great lengths to show his love for us.

The question for us this Advent is this: are we available for God to work in us? Are we patient to wait on his timing, or do we try to take matters into our own hands? Are we completely faithful to him, or do we parcel out our affections to many lesser things? God's jealousy has to do with his love for you. Receive his love anew today and renew your love for him.

Prayer Focus
Memorize and meditate on John 3:16 today:

> *"For God so loved the world that he gave his one and only Son, that whoever believes in him shall not perish but have eternal life."*

4.

In All Things

And my God will meet all your needs according to the riches of his glory in Christ Jesus. To our God and Father be glory for ever and ever. Amen.

Philippians 4:19-20

Could it be that the root of our lack of faith in God is fear? We are afraid that God is not going to come through for us, so we take matters into our own hands. We are afraid that God isn't who he says he is, so we look for things to worship. We don't feel God's presence, so we seek experiences to make up for the need for spiritual expressions. We are afraid that we aren't good enough, smart enough, together enough, or "whatever" enough for God to use us, so we say no to the Spirit's nudges in our hearts.

God's jealousy for us is not only because he demands first place among our priorities but also because he wants us to know the abundant life he offers—to trust that he will meet all of our needs out of his glorious riches. We are precious to God, and he is for us. He wants to be number one in our hearts so that we can fully experience what a life with him offers. And more than that, he wants us to experience the freedom we have in Christ. He wants us to be free of our fears and doubts and anything that holds onto our hearts.

God wants us to know that his plans are always best because he is good and is for us. Remember that throughout the Scriptures the Israelites lacked faith and took matters into their own hands. Repeatedly, the situation got sticky and God redeemed the failed plan of the people. Abraham and Sarah were promised a child, and when the child hadn't come, Sarah schemed with her maidservant to make it happen. Jacob was not happy about being the second-born, so he schemed to take blessings that belonged to Esau. Joseph's brothers did not enjoy the favor shown to Joseph, so they schemed to have him killed. The list goes on, but God always remained faithful, fulfilled his promises, and met their needs. He redeemed the failed plans of his people and restored relationships.

How much more could we experience fullness of life with God if we trust him completely, if we surrender our plans and dreams to him, if we give him our hearts? In the verses that precede our passage for today, Paul writes that he had learned to be content in every circumstance. He had discovered the secret to fullness of life—to trust that God is good and that God loves him beyond measure no matter what situation comes his way.

As we approach Christmas and wait in this Advent season, preparing our hearts for the Christ child, could we dare to believe that God's plans for us are greater than we could imagine? Could we dare to believe that God's jealousy for us is fueled by his love for us and his desire for us to show his love to others? Could we say no to the things that have crowded out room for God in our hearts and let him fill us up with his love and strength? Could we trust that he will meet all of our needs according to his glorious riches?

There's no better time than now to invite God to redeem our failed plans and restore our broken relationships as we put all our hope and trust in his jealous love for us.

Prayer Focus
How are you open to God's leading?

5.

Seek God First

"Therefore I tell you, do not worry about your life, what you will eat or drink; or about your body, what you will wear. Is not life more than food, and the body more than clothes? . . . Your heavenly Father knows that you need them. But seek first his kingdom and his righteousness, and all these things will be given to you as well."

Matthew 6:25, 32-33

What do you "seek first"? When your plans fall through or the check doesn't come or your loved one becomes ill or the pink slip arrives on your desk or your relationship falls apart—to where do you run? Sadly, most of us run to our corners in fear and worry. We let our minds run wild with what-ifs. We ask people to pray for us but never stop to go to the Lord in prayer ourselves.

Jesus knew this about us. He knew that sometimes we seek anything and everything else before we remember to run to him. He knew that we are prone to worry about anything and everything before we remember to trust our needs to the God who gave his only Son for us and promises good gifts to his children. So Jesus gathered his disciples to teach them about trusting God when things are good and when things go bad.

When we stew in our worry and fear instead of running to God, we make an idol of worry; and then we cannot possibly enjoy the fullness of joy that comes from a life with God.

Today's Scripture passage comes in the middle of Jesus' famous Sermon on the Mount. This section of the sermon zeroes in on matters of the heart. Jesus teaches us not to make a show of our religion but to trust that God sees our hearts. He calls us to store up treasures in heaven instead of earthly stuff, and he cuts to the core when he says, "Where your treasure is there your heart will be also" (v. 21). He goes on to challenge our desires by teaching that we can't serve both God and money. In other words, God is jealous—we have to choose between our love of money, things, and God.

Then Jesus turns to the subject of worry because he knows that we struggle with it. Worry is hard to give up. Practically speaking, it seems impossible not to worry. But we don't have to succumb to worry. Jesus invites us to seek him first and trust that everything we need will be provided.

Remember that God is jealous for you and wants your whole heart. Are you bound up in worries and fears this season? Have you spent more time worrying about buying gifts than making room in your life for Jesus? Are you tied up in grief, sadness, or hurt that often surfaces at this time of year? Jesus promises that your heavenly Father knows what you need. "But seek first his kingdom and his righteousness, and all these things will be given to you as well."

God doesn't want to compete with all the things that take your focus off him; he wants to free you from your burdens and cover you with his love, grace, and mercy.

Prayer Focus

What are you worried about today? Seek Jesus.

6.
Be Transformed

Therefore, I urge you, brothers and sisters, in view of God's mercy, to offer your bodies as a living sacrifice, holy and pleasing to God—this is your true and proper worship. Do not conform to the pattern of this world, but be transformed by the renewing of your mind. Then you will be able to test and approve what God's will is—his good, pleasing and perfect will.

Romans 12:1-2

Greed. Lust. Power. Money. Influence. Revenge. Resentment. These are the patterns of the world. The world tells us to get ahead at all costs. Making money and acquiring things are the marks of success, and the general consensus is that "if it feels good and I'm having fun, it's all good"—regardless of what or who gets hurt along the way.

The flip side of that is what the world says about you if you don't match its definition of success and power. The patterns of the world can make us feel less than, put down, and outcast. We begin to believe a narrative that we are not good enough, smart enough, brave enough, or good-looking enough to be accepted. We can begin to wonder what we really have to offer.

So, what does the apostle Paul say about the pattern of this world? "Do not conform." Don't do it. Quit trying to fit in with the ways of the world. Stop your striving. Take off the mask you've been wearing to look the part. Instead, he says, "be transformed by the renewing of your mind." Change the narrative that plays in your mind. Your mind is a powerful muscle that you are in control of. You get to choose what you think about, so Paul says to us change your mind.

We go along in our lives fighting against the current of the culture, but it is so easy to get swept up in it. Especially at Christmastime we have to set our minds on the reason for all the celebrations and parties and gifts. How easy is it to believe the lie that the more gifts you buy equals the better the holiday; or the lie that Christmas is all about store sales and the economy; or even worse, the lie that it doesn't matter that Americans spent about 57 billon dollars on Black Friday last year [2] when it would only cost 10 billion dollars to make sure that the forty percent of the world's population lacking water and sanitation could have access to clean water.[3]

The enemy loves for us to get caught up in the patterns and narratives of the world. But we do not have to be conformed. There is a better way. We can renew our minds, which means to set our minds on God's love, the things God cares about, and the things that please him instead of the things of the world. When our minds are set on God, we have the clarity to see the lies of the world for what they are.

God is jealous for us. He does not want our minds to be set on anything other than his love for us. He does not want to share space in our minds with the deceiver. God is so good and loves us so much that he is for us—he is on our side. God's jealousy is not a punishment but a protection. God wants to protect us from the patterns of the world and the destructive behaviors that go along with them. He wants our minds to filter every single thought through his great love for us. When we do that, we know what is good and pleasing to God.

Sometime over the course of the day, take a minute to write down some of the ways the patterns of the world have taken hold of you. Invite God to renew your mind, to reset it on his goodness. Ask him to help you filter every thought through his love for you and to seek his will this Advent season. Offer your whole self to God as an act of worship—your mind, your heart, your body, your gifts, your bank account—everything, all for him. What a great way to celebrate Christmas this year!

Prayer Focus
What patterns of the world do you struggle with the most? Ask God for the strength to be transformed and set free from those patterns.

7.

Fix Your Eyes

Therefore, since we are surrounded by such a great cloud of witnesses, let us throw off everything that hinders and the sin that so easily entangles. And let us run with perseverance the race marked out for us, fixing our eyes on Jesus, the pioneer and perfecter of faith. For the joy set before him he endured the cross, scorning its shame, and sat down at the right hand of the throne of God. Consider him who endured such opposition from sinners, so that you will not grow weary and lose heart.

Hebrews 12:1-3

In order to run long distances, runners have to let go of unnecessary weight. The goal is to feel light and nimble. Running shoes are made to be as light as possible; running clothes are made to wick away sweat and stay lightweight; water bottles come in lightweight backpacks and belt styles to keep from weighing down runners.

When you think about it, how awful would it be to try to run in heavy clothes, clunky shoes, and backpacks full of gear and water? That run would not feel light and free but heavy and slow.

The writer of Hebrews gives us this picture because he wants to encourage us to run the race of life free from the weight of the world. He wants us to shed anything that gets in the way of our ability to run the race. He says when we hang on to baggage from the past and let it weigh us down, we are to let it go! When we hang on to unmet expectations and succumb to bitterness, we are to let it go! When we get tangled up in something that seemed like a small sin but has wrapped us in a web, we are to let it go! Those things will only cause us to grow weary and lose heart along the way. We have to give them up if we want to make it in the race of life.

All the burdens we carry around with us keep us from a complete focus on God. If we are shifting and struggling with all that weighs us down, our eyes are not focused ahead; instead, they are focused on our struggles.

Remember that God is jealous for us because he loves us so much. He wants all of us, not just the parts of us we feel are presentable. He doesn't want to compete with our attachment to our baggage and the burdens we carry. We don't have to lug that around anymore. In fact, he invites us to bring it to him and be free from it.

The invitation in today's Scripture is to fix your eyes on Jesus. Don't keep looking down at the struggles; look up. Look to Jesus who is cheering you on with all the company of heaven. They are yelling out your name; they are doing "the wave" and calling you forward. Feel the freedom of throwing off anything that hinders your run—the sin, the mixed-up priorities, the baggage, the hurt, the brokenness. Watch them fly away behind you. Feel the wind hit your face and know that God is good. God loves you. God is for you. And then, fix your eyes on Jesus, the baby in the manger in Bethlehem who is the author and perfecter of your faith. This little one is the Peacemaker, the Savior, the Joy-Giver, the Hope of the World. Bring everything you have and everything you are, and lay it down before him. Fix your eyes on him, and let everything else fall away.

Prayer Focus

What weight have you been carrying around that you need to throw off? Invite God to free you from those burdens and give you strength to run without growing weary or losing heart.

WEEK 4
God Is Faithful

1.

Covenant God

As the sun was setting, Abram fell into a deep sleep. . . . When the sun had set and darkness had fallen, a smoking firepot with a blazing torch appeared and passed between the pieces. On that day the LORD made a covenant with Abram.

Genesis 15:12, 17-18a

What a blessing it is to be in a covenant relationship with God, who loves us, always forgives, and stays with us through thick and thin! Even when we neglect the covenant, even when we fail altogether, God loves us. Thanks be to God!

A covenant relationship is one that is more about what you bring to the table than about what the other can do for you. God comes to the covenant with an abundance of love, mercy, and grace to extend; we come with worship, obedience, and trust. We give ourselves to the relationship, not for what we can get out of it but for our love for God and his love for us.

On the other hand, a contract is a service agreement. You make a contract to solidify a give-and-take exchange. It's a payment for a service. When a contract is broken, the agreement is cancelled and the service stopped.

A covenant, though, is a promise to fulfill an oath no matter what the other does or doesn't do. Being in covenant with God means that he will always be faithful to us, no matter when we doubt, distrust, or fail to keep our end of the covenant. God's commitment to us is steady, faithful, and true. The Old Testament is a witness to God's faithfulness when his people neglected and even shunned the covenant yet God still loved them and drew them back. And as we'll discover this week, another witness to God's faithfulness is the manger.

When God spoke to Abram and invited him into a covenant, Abram asked for a sign—something to visually demonstrate the promise. Remember that at this point in time, Abram didn't have any experience of God's faithfulness. He hadn't heard generations of stories about how God had been faithful to his ancestors. He hadn't had multiple encounters in which he had failed God and God had forgiven him. You might wonder why Abram would ask for proof of the covenant, but consider that this was a newly-formed relationship. He didn't have a lot to go on, but you can tell from the passage that Abram wanted to trust God and to enter this covenant.

So Abram asked for a sign, and God provided. God's presence came to Abram as a burning torch that passed through the sacrifices. With this action God essentially said, "I would rather die than break my covenant with you." God was faithful then, and he is still faithful to his promises even now.

We see broken contracts and agreements all day, every day in our world. We are surrounded by a culture of finagling to get the most for ourselves out of contract agreements. This is not a bad thing; contracts are meant to help us ensure we get what we want. We even see marriage covenants treated as contracts and tossed out with the wedding flowers when couples decide they don't want to be married anymore. We are almost numb to news of couples breaking up and calling it quits these days.

God's presence passed through the animal sacrifice, and the message was that God was vowing to keep this covenant. Abram understood that God was promising faithfulness forever.

God's covenant with Abram is God's covenant with us as well. God has promised to be our God; to love us like no one in this world can; to forgive us and remember our sins no more; to redeem our lives from the pit of emptiness; to give us life abundant; to break into our world; to know us, save us, and die for us so that we might live. Our God is a covenant God.

Prayer Focus
What are you giving to your covenant relationship with God?

2.

God Remembers

"Can a mother forget the baby at her breast
and have no compassion on the child she has borne?
Though she may forget,
I will not forget you!
See, I have engraved you on the palms of my hands."

Isaiah 49:15-16a

Imagine the scene: Max is in the second grade. The bell has rung, and his classmates have gathered their things to wait in the carpool line. One by one, his friends' names are called, and Max watches them run out the door. When the line starts dwindling down, Max notices that there are only a few kids left to be called. One at time the last few children head out the door, excited to hop into their cars and go home. Finally, Max is the only one left. No cars are waiting in line. The extra teachers helping with the car line have gone back to their rooms. It's just Max and his teacher waiting for his mom to come. Max begins to cry, wondering where his mom is. Did she forget him? Is she OK? Will she ever come? Is he in trouble? When will she get here? His crying turns to weeping as he is now convinced that he will live at the school forever. He is forgotten, or so he thinks.

Of course, his mom has not forgotten him. She is running late and has been caught in traffic. She is frantic in her quest to reach the school. She loves her son and would hate for him to feel forgotten or sad. A mother could never forget her child.

How many of us have been Max and felt abandoned and forgotten? How many of us have been the mom who did not get there at the expected time despite our efforts to reach our child?

The Israelites struggled to keep their covenant with God. The Old Testament is full of their up-and-down commitment to God. However, God was always faithful—always working for their good, even when they didn't see it. At one point they felt forgotten and alone. But God reminded them that just as a mother could never forget the baby she carried in her womb, so God would never forget his love for them. No matter how far away from God they might walk or what kind of messes they might make, God would never leave them alone. God is a faithful God. He would work all things together for their good, even though they wouldn't always see his hand at work. Throughout Scripture we learn more about what it means that God is faithful. The story is one of a faithful God and an unfaithful people.

Have you ever felt forgotten, abandoned, or hopeless, as if God were absent? Know this: God sees you, hears your cries, and is for you. God has made a covenant of faithfulness to you. Though you may not feel him or see him, God is keeping his covenant of faithfulness even now. Just as little Max was not forgotten or abandoned when he sat waiting on his mom, we can be sure that we are always on God's mind, even when we think he is late. God is never late but always working in our lives for our good. God is faithful and dependable and true.

As you walk closer to the manger this week, consider that Jesus is a sign of the promise fulfilled—God's covenant fulfilled in the newborn babe. You are not alone or forgotten. The God of the universe stepped down into our world to embrace you, to claim you, to assure you that you will never, ever, be forgotten. No matter where you've been, what you've done, or how far you've run, God is faithful. You have a home in him. God sees you. God remembers his covenant to you, and he would rather die than break that covenant.

Prayer Focus

When have you felt forgotten? Invite God to cover you in confidence that you are never alone.

3.

The Lord Saves

"Do not be afraid. I bring you good news that will cause great joy for all the people. Today in the town of David a Savior has been born to you; he is the Messiah, the Lord."

Luke 2:10-11

Can you hear Linus as he stands, blanket in hand, on the stage next to that sad, little Christmas tree reciting Luke 2? In the middle of their mess of a Christmas play, an exasperated Charlie Brown declares that nobody knows what Christmas is all about anymore. Even the cartoon character is disturbed by the commercialization and rampant consumerism of Christmas. But Linus knows what Christmas is all about, and he focuses the Peanuts crew back to what really matters this season: Jesus. That's what Christmas is all about.

In the midst of our crazy schedules, shopping lists, work parties, and travel plans, Jesus comes to us as a sign of God's everlasting, never-giving-up kind of love. As we, like Charlie Brown's friends, get lost in the consumerism and commercialization, the God of the universe breaks into our world to save us. An angel announces that there is "good news that will cause great joy for all the people." Jesus comes as the fulfillment of an ancient promise and a sign of God's forever faithfulness. His arrival is good news for the world.

God's people had seen judges, kings, prophets, counselors, and healers; but those people had only exposed their lack of ability to keep the covenant. What they really needed—and what we need—is a Savior, and God provided just that. Why do we celebrate Christmas? Because God sent a Savior who is the Messiah, Christ the Lord.

God gave us laws, but we couldn't keep them. God gave us prophets, but we sent them away. So God gave us his Son, who would be born into this world for the sole purpose of saving our lives. We are incapable of paying for our sin. But God, who is rich in mercy and love, stepped down into our time and space to pay the penalty for sin. The baby born in Bethlehem would grow up to lead us to God and ultimately tear down the barrier of sin and death. He would die so that we could live forever with him.

Our human understanding might lead us to conclude that God abandoned Jesus as he died on the cross. We might assume that God didn't love him enough or that he had given up on us all. But the truth of the matter is that the cross shows us just how much God loves you and me. Jesus came to earth and died on a cross because God is faithful to keep his promises.

As you go about your Christmas preparations, vacation plans, and activities, hear the angels call to you with their good news. A Savior has been born for you. He will forgive you. He will heal you. He will give you abundant and eternal life. He will restore you. He will show you what faithfulness means.

Prayer Focus

How have you known God's faithfulness in your life?

4.
God's Promises

As far as the east is from the west,
so far has he removed our transgressions from us.

Psalm 103:12

"Never will I leave you;
never will I forsake you."

Hebrews 13:5b

"I will not leave you as orphans; I will come to you."

John 14:18

And my God will meet all your needs according to the
riches of his glory in Christ Jesus.

Philippians 4:19

If you were to make a mental list of the promises of God, what would make the list? What promises do you call to mind when you need to recall God's faithfulness?

God's promises point to his faithfulness from generation to generation. The heart of the gospel is God's faithfulness to keep his promises. God's promise to send a Rescuer—one who would set things right, demonstrate his sacrificial love, and blot out sin and death once and for all—came through the little baby in Bethlehem. The Rescuer had come, and God was ready to tell the whole world.

The promise is this: God will not remember our transgressions. The psalmist declares that God removes them as far as the east is from the west. God's faithful love is expressed by his one-hundred-percent forgiveness. He doesn't hold onto our mistakes so that he can use them against us. No, he blots them out entirely. God is faithful to remember our sins no more.

The promise is this: God will never leave you or forsake you. In this world, you may feel alone and abandoned. People will fail you, turn on you, disappoint you, hurt you, and leave you for dead. But God won't. God sees you. He loves you. He knows you. He is for you. You are not alone. God is faithful to be present with you anywhere and everywhere.

The promise is this: God will not leave you to fend for yourself. You will not be without a great Caregiver and Guardian. This world may leave you lost and alone. You may have no one looking out for you, no one on your side, no one caring for your needs. But God is your loving Father and Provider. God is your family. You are not alone. You are never alone in this world. God is faithful to care for you.

The promise is this: Every need you will ever have is found in the glorious riches of Jesus Christ. You may be at the end of your rope, the end of your bank account, the end of your hope, or the end of your joy; but God will meet your needs. God is faithful to take care of you.

Are you without hope this Advent? Are you lost and feeling alone? There is a promise from God for you: you are never alone. You are loved and known. God came down to earth so you would know the depth of his great love for you.

Memorize these promises and let them permeate your life. God is faithful to fulfill each and every one!

Prayer Focus

Memorize one or two of today's Scripture promises.

5.

The Backstory

"I, the L<small>ORD</small> *, have called you in righteousness;*
I will take hold of your hand.
I will keep you and will make you
to be a covenant for the people
and a light for the Gentiles,
to open eyes that are blind,
to free captives from prison
and to release from the dungeon those
who sit in darkness."
Isaiah 42:6-7

Have you ever tried to walk in on a movie that has already started or to jump into a television series mid-season? It can be extremely difficult to pick up on the backstory and understand the humor or plot when you didn't watch from the beginning. For today's Scripture passage, you can only understand the context of God's message if you know the backstory.

Here is a quick history review to set the scene for these words of Isaiah. God rescued the Israelites from slavery in Egypt. He had made a covenant with them to be their God and direct their path. He brought them out of the wilderness and to the Promised Land. They built a Temple and a city, and they built their lives around God— for a while.

Various kings led them to some victories and also some defeats. They went back and forth between faithfulness and rebellion for years until the prophets of God came to speak truth and wisdom, calling them to repent and return to God. But then they were defeated by the Babylonians. Around the sixth century B.C., their Temple was destroyed, their belongings were taken from them, and they became slaves in Babylon.

This was the depth of despair. How could this be? How could God abandon his people after saving them so many times? The Israelites had lost hope and their memory of the promises of God. They could not recall the faithfulness of God. They wondered why God had forsaken them after such a long journey. They may have even questioned God's goodness. They were at the end of their strength.

This is the backstory for this passage of Isaiah. So this section of Isaiah was meant to bring to mind the faithfulness of God and remind God's people of the good things God had done.

God called his people to look to him, to be hopeful, and to wait. God declared his promises once again to his people, and they listened, weighted down with grief and despair.

God's word came as hope. God was with his people, working on their behalf, and God invited them to join in his justice-seeking work. God had not forgotten them; they were not alone or abandoned. They would be restored and remain firmly on the other side of a covenant with God that cannot be broken.

Rescue was on the way. God would send a servant to fulfill his promises once and for all. Jesus would be the fulfillment of the promise. Jesus would be the servant God sent to make his people a light to the nations—even those who were outside the covenant—to open God's realm to everyone, to open the eyes of the blind, to set the captive free, and to carry the light to the darkest corners of the world. If you know Jesus' story, then you know that he proclaimed this mission at his baptism. Jesus' first words of ministry were these words from the book of Isaiah.

Do you see the theme of faithfulness? Even when God's people were at their lowest point and sure of their defeat, God spoke hope and reset their vision on his faithfulness.

Have you ever wondered where God was or what he was up to? Have you felt tricked or abandoned? Here's the thing that is so difficult to remember: God is always at work and is always faithful, even when we don't see or understand his ways. God's character is faithfulness. He cannot be conniving. He cannot be manipulative. He cannot trick you. It is not his nature. It is not his character. No, he is faithful. Our God is faithful and true, and he is working for our good when we see his hand and when we don't.

In these final days of Advent, consider that God is faithful to you all the time—when you see his hand and when you wonder what he is doing. Look at the manger and remember that God fulfills his promises. He does what he says he will do.

Prayer Focus

When have you felt abandoned? How can you learn to trust God no matter what comes your way?

6.
In the Family

But when the fulfillment of the time came, God sent his Son, born through a woman, and born under the Law. This was so he could redeem those under the Law so that we could be adopted. Because you are sons and daughters, God sent the Spirit of his Son into our hearts, crying, "Abba, Father!" Therefore, you are no longer a slave but a son or daughter, and if you are his child, then you also are an heir through God.

Galatians 4:4-7 CEB

In yesterday's Scripture reading we heard God foretell a coming servant who would be a light to the Gentiles—to all nations. We learned that God's covenant would extend beyond the Hebrew people. Today we hear from the apostle Paul that we are all children of God. We are adopted into the family. In fact, there is no separation between biological children and adopted kids. No, Paul says that we are all adopted into God's family as heirs in Jesus Christ. Through Jesus, we are in the family of God—you and me! We get to experience the wonder of being in covenant with God. As Jesus calls God his *Abba*, his Daddy, so we are invited into a sweet, intimate, Daddy-child relationship with God.

We are only a few days from Christmas morning. You no doubt have already exchanged a few gifts and sung a few Christmas carols. Most likely your lights are hung, your tree is lit, the packages are wrapped—you have this Christmas just about under wraps.

As you approach the manger this year, consider what it all means to you. Does it mean a silent night and Christmas candy? Does it mean Santa Claus and stockings hung with care? Does it mean breakfast casserole and Christmas ham? Or does it mean God is faithful? Does it mean God is a promise-keeper? Does it mean God is a good and loving Father who gives good gifts to his children? Does it mean Love came down at Christmastime?

We don't usually hear much from Paul during Christmas. We hear from the prophets foretelling Jesus' arrival and we hear the story of the nativity in the Gospels, but maybe today is just the day to lean into Paul's words about who and whose we are. Paul's words speak to our very identity. We are in God's family. Once we were far from God, but God has come close and adopted us into his family. Through Jesus Christ we are heirs to all the riches of heaven. We are beloved. We are wanted. We are known. We are family.

God is faithful. God's covenant love extends from Abram to you and me. The invitation into the covenant means that we get to experience the unconditional, forever love of God. He is a for-better-or-worse kind of God. He is a till-death-do-us-part kind of God. He is forever faithful.

Adoption is not a temporary arrangement. Adoption is a permanent transfer of identity. Where we once were enemies of God, we are now welcomed into his family permanently.

The Christmas season often brings joy and gratitude for all that God has done; it also can bring melancholy, sadness, and depression at times. For some reason, the season often causes hurts to rise from the surface and broken hearts to feel the pangs of pain again. In these struggles, we can forget our identity. We can forget that we belong to Someone.

Instead of forgetting, let us choose to let go instead. We can let go of our guilt. We can let go of our shame. We can let go of our fears. We can let go of our hurt. We can let go of our baggage. We are free from our past, and we have a bright future as beloved children of God!

Prayer Focus

Thank God for adopting you into his family and inviting you to call him Daddy.

7.

See What Great Love

See what great love the Father has lavished on us, that we should be called children of God! And that is what we are!

1 John 3:1

At the end of the Advent journey we arrive here at 1 John 3:1 to "see what great love the Father has lavished on us." What a fitting end to an Advent journey. The transition from Advent to Christmas comes with a realization that God the Father lavishes love upon his children in the form of his only Son.

This gift is not one we can earn. We can't pray our way to the manger. We can't serve our way there either. In fact, we can't work for it at all. God has lavished us with a gift beyond compare. He has broken into the world to lead us back to him—to break down any walls and claim us as his own.

Imagine the father of a newborn baby. He looks on with intense anticipation as his wife labors. He cries with joy as he gets the first look at the baby. He lovingly tends to the baby while mom is tended to by nurses. He proudly carries the baby down the hallway to the waiting room and announces his or her arrival. He is proud. He is a father. This is the moment he gets to tell everyone the news. That child will never have to wonder who Dad is. The father lavishes love upon the child so that the child's identity is bound up in the father's love.

Likewise, our very identity is bound up in God's love for us. We don't earn it; instead, God lavishes it—pours it out—on us.

Look at the declaration: "and that is what we are!" Some translators even include an exclamation point to give it that extra oomph. It is declared: we are children of God.

In this world we have trouble. Jesus promised it would be so. Friends disappoint us. Bosses let us go. Spouses betray us. These moments can be excruciating. We can begin to wonder if we can count on anyone, if we matter to anyone, if we can trust anyone. We can forget who we are and to whom we belong.

But the writer of today's Scripture reminds us that God not only calls us his children; he makes us his children. He has done all the work of adoption and given us the gift of his divine family. Because of this truth, we can have all the assurance that God is faithful, true, sure, and full of love. If you have ever struggled with the assurance of your salvation and adoption into God's family, claim this promise today: you are a child of God!

From the beginning of time, God has been faithfully working all things together for the good of his beloved children. He has lived out his end of the covenant and fulfilled every promise he has made. He has planned and prepared and sent a Rescuer to announce his kingdom and fully make us his own. After years of prophecies, the people looked and waited and watched for the Messiah to come. And then, when an angel appeared to Mary, God's plan was set in motion.

Mary and Joseph, Zechariah and Elizabeth, the angel Gabriel, the shepherds, the wise men, the heavenly hosts—all participate in the story of God's lavish display of love for you and for me. The promise of a Messiah, of a Savior, was coming true. The Savior of the world had come to prove the wonders of God's love.

Every day in this Advent journey we have explored God's character—God is expectant, dangerous, jealous, and above all, faithful. We have witnessed through the Scriptures the ways that God has reached out to us, drawn us to himself, and demonstrated his great love for us. And today, we close with a gift we never expected. The gift is wrapped in swaddling clothes and hidden away in a barn in Bethlehem. In this gift there is no darkness at all, only unconditional love, grace, mercy, forgiveness, and adoption into the family of God. What an amazing gift, and what an amazing Gift-giver.

Come to the manger and see what love the Father has lavished on us. Come and open your gift, receive the gift with joy, and live in covenant with the God who is forever faithful.

Prayer Focus
Thank God that you are called his child.

Christmas: A Season of Joy

There were sheepherders camping in the neighborhood. They had set night watches over their sheep. Suddenly, God's angel stood among them and God's glory blazed around them. They were terrified. The angel said, "Don't be afraid. I'm here to announce a great and joyful event that is meant for everybody, worldwide: A Savior has just been born in David's town, a Savior who is Messiah and Master. This is what you're to look for: a baby wrapped in a blanket and lying in a manger."

At once the angel was joined by a huge angelic choir singing God's praises:

Glory to God in the heavenly heights,
Peace to all men and women on earth who please him.

Luke 2:8-14 THE MESSAGE

The news of Mary's pregnancy was at first curious and scary, but Mary quickly moved to a place of joy at the wonder of what God would do in her. From that moment until Jesus finally arrived and the angels sang out over fields of sheep, calling to the shepherds, there was joy. Joy began the story, and joy cried out as Jesus was born. God has fulfilled his covenant, rescued his people, and come to live among us.

So many emotions and feelings go along with the Christmas season, but perhaps the truest expression of the season is joy. Joy knows that the grace of Jesus covers every sin of the past. Joy knows that every hurt can find a comfort in Jesus. Joy knows that every sickness can find restoration in Jesus. Joy knows that every unmet expectation can find fulfillment in Jesus. Love has come; joy to the world!

As you celebrate Christmas again this year, soak in the joy. Don't let the season pass you by without slowing down and savoring the joy that God has brought into your life. While the world tries to get you worked up and frantic at all there is to do, slow down and rest in the arms of a God who is all you'll ever need. When the world tries to tell you that material gifts prove love, remember the joy of receiving the gift of Jesus.

God is eager to give you the gift of himself. He is eager for you to open up the gift and find the abundant life that awaits you when you make yourself completely available to God. So go ahead, open up the gift. Receive the gift of Jesus anew in your heart. Live with fullness of joy and hope and peace because Love has come to make a home in your heart.

Prayer Focus
Celebrate the gift of Jesus!

Notes

1. "O Little Town of Bethlehem," Phillips Brooks, 1868, *The United Methodist Hymnal* (Nashville: The United Methodist Publishing House, 1989), 230.

2. "Black Friday Spending Falls Despite Record Crowds," http://www.huffingtonpost.com/2013/12/02/black-friday-spending -falls_n_4371104.html;

3. "Price of Safe Water for All," http://www.nytimes.com/2000 /11/23/world/price-of-safe-water-for-all-10-billion-and-the -will-to-provide-it.html.